Snare

poems by

Elisa Karbin

Finishing Line Press
Georgetown, Kentucky

Snare

Copyright © 2018 by Elisa Karbin
ISBN 978-1-63534-500-1 First Edition
All rights reserved under International and Pan-American Copyright Conventions.
No part of this book may be reproduced in any manner whatsoever without written permission from the publisher, except in the case of brief quotations embodied in critical articles and reviews.

ACKNOWLEDGMENTS

I'm grateful to the editors of the following publications in which versions of these poems have appeared:

Crab Orchard Review: "Summer Squall"
Tinderbox Poetry Journal: "Revision In Studio," "An Interpretation of Dreams," "Deep Spring"
Stirring: A Literary Collective: "Modern History"

My endless gratitude to my family and the University of Wisconsin-Milwaukee poetry community for their support, keen criticism and mentorship: especially Rebecca Dunham and Meredith Barber.

Thanks also to the Culeen and James Siebert and the Vermont Studio Center for the space and time to write.

Publisher: Leah Maines

Editor: Christen Kincaid

Cover Art and Design: Meredith Barber

Author Photo: Kristin Sczepanski

Printed in the USA on acid-free paper.
Order online: www.finishinglinepress.com
also available on amazon.com

Author inquiries and mail orders:
Finishing Line Press
P. O. Box 1626
Georgetown, Kentucky 40324
U. S. A.

Table of Contents

Revision in Studio 1

Interpretation of Dreams 2

Metamorphosis 3

The Girl with the Rag in Her Mouth 4

Deep Spring 5

Thrall 6

Playing Dead 7

Modern History 8

Ideation 9

Dear X, From the Spoil 10

In Medias Res 11

May Day 12

Prelude 13

Summer Squall 14

Melancholia 15

The Girl with Her Eyes Sewn Shut 16

Anniversary Reaction 17

Fragment 18

Conjuration at Pacific Beach 19

I: 20

The Daughter 21

The Girl with Her Hands Full of Loam 22

Raptus 23

for
Jessica, Sara & Alexa
This is words.

"Why does tragedy exist? Because you are full of rage. Why are you full of rage? Because you are full of grief."

Anne Carson, *Grief Lessons: Four Plays by Euripides*

REVISION IN STUDIO

This morning, light fell onto my page
same as it did in the room I was once
pinned to.   Identical, the slant and slice
of gold, the smell of spring's breath,
musk of a foreign body's lope and lurk.
I am pinioned beneath the weight of him
still—I think it will be a thousand
more sleeplessnesses before I can creep
my way out from under his heft, the hands
clasping the red of my lips, sealing the damp
tinge of my tongue—   Pelvis bored
to mine, I am always straddled supine,
wrestled over until, like falling, I am weightless;
a reed-boned bird, a blind and diving bird.
    Most days I can make the bed
a raft, him a trailing sinker around my neck.
It's the opening eye that is the problem—
the unfurling of the moment that seizes me
by the throat and shakes.   This morning
the poem on the page was a love poem to my
skin. No—an ode to how I bit and clawed, or
an elegy to my guilty body, breaking in waves,
a new crack for every year; a eulogy.

AN INTERPRETATION OF DREAMS

Where have I gone from:
        Room of rot.
  Dim, waterlogged celluloid.
    Salted brine-dark room,
       somewhere close to sea.
Unwindowed room.
    Room far by crow-call from
      my land-locked father.

How to say I want to return
    from where I never knew
      I was— Girl sewn
to the window's seam; Girl hemmed
      to the keyhole's hollow: Is this
coming through in the transmission?
    My end is static: Slush
     and snow from the telephone
line creeping like thistle in the yard.
      Slush and static, the image
  warping in the dark
    nest of my thorny sleep.

Somewhere in the deep of me
    I've buried the lock to the cellar,
     the soot-singed engine-room
   of memory's looming furnace. Somewhere
behind the thrumming lick of the mirror's blank surface
    the girl playing dead
  has pinched her lips white,
  has swallowed a key.

METAMORPHOSIS

A hail of white fury and Cygnus appears.
      Specter through sea-fog, time slows
in the arc of his flight, in the swift hammer
      of his wing-flap.   Seconds count
no sound. Each shapeless moment unspools
      in the thunder's tungsten overhead,
tendrils like blood over her foraged body.
      Anointed, she is a roped red offering.
Girl bound by the plait of terror's mute curse.

Unvoiced, she is made quiet by the swirling
      current, by the dive and thrust of the
swan-blur into her. Slow friction burns her raw.
      Heat of particles, spark of static's gray
swirl—swelling summer's permanent dusk.

This, the chemistry that hastens cumulonimbus
      lightning fields, the electric remnant of his
hot desire's flashing charge.   In the slow drum
      of time's return she moves her mouth, shapes
her tongue around the roiling crest of a thunderhead
      on the horizon;   Her breath is a rushing
echo, the crack of collision: Atomic, elemental.

      She wakes with a hollow throat: This,
the weight of the vacated body;
      the presence gone, light passing through.

THE GIRL WITH THE RAG IN HER MOUTH

        never cries out. Instead,
bites down, tastes the brine
              of salt gnashed

        into her teeth. Hard
grit. Agony's centuries sealed
              between her lips.

        Like devotion, the red
of her guilt is an ember
              glowing in her gut, is

        the red running
thick from her tongue. The girl
              with the rag in her mouth

        is let up from the bed,
is untied from the bedsheets,
              to be stripped of her skin.

DEEP SPRING

It wasn't that
streaming like an ablution
I couldn't say no to
the smell of boy.
Sweat and
around us
the falling moon
but in the shadow
I never used to be
so soiled
dark
ready to,
mouth, claw
I wanted to but
It was
always
me,

I wanted to but somehow
through the half-closed window
the dirt under your fingernails,
The husk of your body
the blood on your teeth shone.
All of it shook me:
reflected blankly
a blackened wing
so coy.
I was fecund,
humming spring
like poppies
upward from
a fist
your heft that made me
quail and shake.
like sickness

in the bath of blue light
like a damp spectral sheet
your wild-eye gleam
rapped my eyelids.
Saliva clasped to the air
The light washed,
across my body
whittled dark in the dissolve.
So full of loam and wet,
green like the chattering
I vibrated with yes, yes, yes
sprouted from the
inside. It's not that
I could not bear it. You
beat my thighs—
Your thickness inside
was never welcome.

THRALL

The ghost of my skin   arises,
tinder for his   want. I am un-

    latched from the bed I
was laid on—   from the mouth

that fed   on my bones,   licked
clean the blood from   my eyes.

I've tried to sew   myself into
the mattress spring's   rust, to tie

myself   to the seam of the pillow's
    plush. But I'm   pulled, tooth

from socket, from   my body   when I
feel the crack   of his   skin against

mine, his soot-   stench breath   on
my breast, ash   fingers lanced through me.

PLAYING DEAD

So she sleeps. Lead-heavy, her belly
rises and falls. Each scrape of breath
is night, a scarf given wind by her lips.

She sleeps and is made fitful by dreams:
a cold looming dusk, a coarse shadow
laced through her in her dreamed

body—the one untangled by appetites
that are not hers, the body unfettered
by ropes of want, the grotesque hunger

of desire.   She sleeps and is made
light like the untethered moon hanging ripe
beyond the treeline; the tawny eye of god

burning through winter's black mask, its glint
a cypher of lullabies rasped through the dark.

MODERN HISTORY

It was nothing like mythology—you
did not appear to me in a meadow
in the body of a swan, in the shape
of a bull. My hair was unadorned
with laurel or rose;   Yes, a lick
of the sea clung to the air, hung
like a curtain or a mourning cloak,
shivered its hem along the tops of
burnt-black trees, grazed the slats
of the painted pine headboard.
    No god's arrow sliced through
the silence, only the sound of the
ice cubes' slow reduction in their glass
tumblers, only the feel of your skin
on mine—unfeathered, unfurred,
a scrabble of thorns barbing my soft
belly, the thatch of my mons, deeper.
    No, I can't recall the whisper
of your seduction, only the rasping
grunt of angry friction. The honeyed
wine was cheap and burned. It didn't
unpetal me but tore through like a black
fire, singed a hole in my pit and you,
neither god nor man, crawled in
to claim me.   Maybe it was
like mythology—Undressed, my skin
became a constellation of purple
and puce. Every mirror I faced
was met with a body transformed—
sloped like a curse, hung like a limp
flag of conquest, blanched and waiving
under fluorescent lights. Forged
in blood and rage, my reflection
became a screaming idol, unmoved
by your name, uneffaced by your touch.

IDEATION

Recall's heat comes in surges—Sulfurous,
                a murmuration of starlings

stirring in my empty chest. This red-bone
              holler swarms and threads

through capillary and vein, is pumped out
                  by the engine of my surly

heart.   Stanch it. Stop its black-winged
                  surge, a raw and vicious spill

making my gut a raucous lake. Seductive in its
                coil and pull, its call to drown.

Outside the raw-rubbed skin of trauma's
                cut—this clean psychic gash—

birds are shaking off their feathered moorings
                setting out to wing across my

body's shore. Each wingshadow rakes a tiding
              wave, a small rebellion. Darkly

these starlings trail across the skein of me as if
              a rupture, another blade dragging.

DEAR X, FROM THE SPOIL

Like the blue unraveled from the leaded
dusk, I am unstitched again, awake and listening
to the sounds of thunderheads dragging
their gray through the bleeding red of day's
slow fading into night. It is always the same:
the pinpricked scars of rain mottle my body,
wither me like the thrums of guilt stitched hot
in my veins. The bitter slip of pills
chalk my tongue, makes metallic every taste
of rain I try to drink.   I have not forgotten
you. I have not finished with your soot-wet
scent, your filthy breath; I'm unspooled by
your dark snare and pull, by your strangling
heat binding my bones, tacking my eyelids closed.

IN MEDIAS RES

Again, the hour counts down. My good doctor's
lamplight is a static sun I watch. The humming
filament tarries its light, steady, immovable in its
resolve to stay lit despite the genuine glinting
through the black slats, half-closed; a gesture toward
the intimate nature of revelations.
                                                  Yes, trauma. Yes,
the pier. In this room I conjure the black murumuration,
the friction and frenzy like a dust cloud kicked into
the face of the fading sun. How my eyes stung for hours
after. To be clear, not like the ringing salt-heat of tears.
No, I recall the blunt shock of my own face's dull
reflection in the bathroom mirror, my own face rain-
glazed, ghosting the puddles of the parking lot I walked
to find a bus.
                But this isn't right. I don't want to start
in medias res—I want the whole of it said and out of me,
and at once. Not a piecemeal collage, the horror-show
vignettes of time's carnival hall. I want the certainty and fact,
the weights and figures spoken as a record. I want to remember
what I do not want to recall.
                                    My doctor and I agree: the process
takes time. I must conduct my own unraveling, undress myself.

MAY DAY

Incongruous, the day rends itself apart,
        separated like the lobes of the brain's
hemispheres—which glisten like dew
        on grass, which shiver like wind's rushing
through the roseroot's nap—Unintelligible,
        the day tries to speak, but split,
it is palsied, immutable and dumb
        as a dead purpled tongue, as the knot
in my chest, my pulping heart
        full of dull fire.

Like gravity I have sunk again—
        my veins tighten. The cold cloudiness
of my gunpowder-thin skin strains
        to hold me under the weight of my vicious
blood, my venomous, clotting-sun
        red blood. Snap of synapse, the clasp
of guilt is wrung around me like dawn
        falling on the finch's green wing, or
through me the way the sun, in its tilt,
        ruptures the leaded curtain of night, drives
forward the needling of stars, the needling
        of each half-closed eye.

PRELUDE

Start with the pier stretched like skin
                    spun from fingers threaded through
         hush and viscera. The weft of waves
blueing the skyline, what we can make
                of skyline, given
                the wet ink of water,
the salted canvas of sky.
                        Enter us—we
    are the we here—I am standing with my
palms pressed to the boardwalk's slick
              rail, not holding on, not letting go. I am
too callow, too love-struck to be afraid.
                You with your shirtless ease,
                your predator's lope in tight
                jeans, pronouncing my name
so casually it feels like a kiss.
                    Later, you'll say my name again,
        you'll stretch it like a carnival song,
                the warped disc of your voice
will echo in the unlit room, will tangle
            in my knotted hair, skim across the rising
bruise of my mouth when I gasp awake, when
        you cover the mirror and ask me to leave.

SUMMER SQUALL

Here summer's salt and swelter hastens
the divide—this milky pith between sky
and sea is a wound cauled by crow-call,
packed in the soot of memory's residue.
The brain stalls in the blue-black
scatter of fragmented moments: Sleep's
rough touch is a rope knotted by night,
pulling each lighted moment of before,
after, and the after.
          Quietly, the body rebels.
Muscles strain against the slippage, this
strange falling back. Muscles strain. Remember
the starched certainty of surrender. Remember
the storm-wrecked harbor this body is now.

Dear Interrupted Echo, my tessellate twin:
This is the intersection of living and the ghost-
crept ache to stop. Atomic certainty's already
grown its mountain in the gut.
                              The best way
to die is to be still among the riot.   Be waveless
kneeling in the raw white of swirling surf. Lay.
Find comfort in the spitting ire of the sure current,
                    in the claw and coil of forgetting.

MELANCHOLIA

    Scattered among my own
litany of loss, I have made myself
a hermetic thing, sealed my eyes

    against the moon's bright-
cut brilliance, to the sun's gold clutch
swelling.   I have been restless,

    waited patient with my own
reckonings; I've sewn silt to the seams
of my every dress, thrashed headless

    against the stone-mouthed rictus
of the river's ridge until my fingers tangled
the rush, until my meat grayed chalksoft in

    the sediment bed.   Once, I
longed for a lacuna, to drown and wake
clear-eyed among the dead. My becoming

    as Persephone reborn—I, lush
revision of spring: body an unmarshalled
font, a ripened orchard.   There is no

    resurrection without prayer
and mine have been said breathless—
His curse-kiss still stings my mouth,
his hands still yoked around my throat.

THE GIRL WITH HER EYES SEWN SHUT

waits under the hem of her
mother's swelled dress, counting

the seconds of sunlight streaming
through the lace, the scored silk,

the eyelet edge.   The girl
with her eyes sewn shut smells

cirrus, cumulonimbus on her tongue,
the wash of light warm on her breast.

    Then the raven's wing, soot
of his shadow ties its noose about

her throat, rips his claws into her frock,
bites the nape of her neck until

she is wrestled down, carried like smoke
to the thorn and snare of his nest.

ANNIVERSARY REACTION

Soot-wet, I smell him. My snare
my black-breath man, hanging
in my gut. Unwelcome
pendulum. He shades the corners,
of me, the deep, unswept places.

> No— that is wrong because
> the night rives from its glassy shell,
> rains itself down— a litter of
> snuffed out stars, blank shadows of birds.

Awake, light blanches night's black-licked
tongue. Awake, I can turn my hand to a fist,
bite and claw at the catch of another's skin.
Wakefulness, this sterile place. I mourn its
gossamer smoke, its transience. And so, one
must learn to cope with the night-brought haunt:

> *No reproach:*
> guilt is an old blue bird: do not
> mill your breath to seed and feed it.
> *Breathe deep:*
> unless to breathe becomes
> a grasping cord of hands
> to choke you.
> *Don't seek him:*
> he will be married now. He will have become
> fatted and content. In his bald happiness
> he will not look capable.

Now, the silt of stars strain through
the unwashed window, the unkempt bed
marked with blood, with the ash-black
blot of his ravenous wing. Make note:
your tongue is the clench of quicksand;
the rooms you walk melt underfoot.

FRAGMENT

I wake   next to me   his body
    telegraphing   cinder-signals
awash   purple light,   the cracked open
    dawn   airplane drag   overhead
his soot breath   each pull through   air
    a knife across wet paper   my skin
soft   vellum   ripe under his touch
    I   the laden fruit he sucked
raw   the red of his mouth   chaps me   all
    over the tremble   and shake the snarl
of his hands   then   sickness
    waves breaking   shore of my lips
a salted wound   acridity of vomit   fog
    in the mirror   blue   his iris burnt through me

CONJURATION AT PACIFIC BEACH

The words I cast into the pitch-purled dark echoed like hands striking, like the clench of a fist around the stalk of a neck. Feral, the crack and snap of what I meant to say filled the hollow space between my lips—   No one told me grief, its red-black wing, its needle throat, is a caesura, a slipping sideways into the barrel of loss, existence in the pocket of space between the fingers curled toward an empty palm.   .   Unmagic, I can conjure the husks of doves, a rabbit's paw, moments captured on memory's fickle mercury film: cotton-licked shins, his hand knotting my spine, the saccharine tang of seaglass smoothed to a luster beneath my feet—rough snag of my skin in my slipping.   Poppy bright, blood bloomed where his bite and lick lingered, suffused the glassy shallows.

                                              The white of a scar bloomed.

I:

wild fire: my brain: bound, speechless,
to flame: tether of smoke rises
in my blood: call it by its name: unknown:
call it: melancholia: cursive stroke of block-
lettered maladies: course through me:
my skin is white: vellum, washed over:
palimpsest: trauma: now, the retelling:
I was walking along the banks of a river:
I was walking along the teeth of a lake: I:
a hook-mouthed trout sent skyward in
seizure: out of water: too long: bring me
the baptismal font: a homecoming: drape
me in the white gown: devotion: waiving
wings of a holy ghost: let me divide myself:
my gristle and gills: my cells: exquisite cancer.

THE DAUGHTER

        Where have you gone to, soot-breath man?
        Dormant under my skin so long, I feel you
           always. Black charm albatrossed
                around my neck. My mouth still crowned
from your kiss; your heat's a bitterness laced
        through me. Like a haunt,
           you efface me.

Strange symmetry: Making in the unmaking;
the viciousness of one hand quickens into a fist,
        the other curling to a lull
        around your sleeping child.

The brute grip of irony isn't lost on me.
        Not that I could have been precious,
        not that I could have been clean. Your violence
is inevitable, ineffable as her monstrous wails.

        She has not yet learned the language of trauma.
One day she will know.
        She will come to you
        with a palsied tongue, she will come to you
and not be her own. You know the world is cruel,
because it harbors a home for you, for men
        like you; slight gods in men's clothes,
to take and keep whatever small thing they survey.

        What is a body to you if not a shell, a stone,
           an apple to bite to the core and toss?

One day your daughter will pronounce a name.
        It will sound like yours, it won't be yours. It will
be wet and cold and it will fall in a smear at your
        feet like a dull, pulping heart.

        You will not know with what hand to hold it;
        You will not know how to put it back.
        You will understand that you can't.

THE GIRL WITH HER HANDS FULL OF LOAM

tries to bury herself every night
by the glow of a tumescent yellow
moon, its glare like an eye seeping

through the spaces of her teeth,
between each vertebrae bent in
supplication to the god who whispers

dig here and splay your heart, dig here,
protract your bones. The girl with her hands
full of loam obeys each time. The girl

with her hands full of loam dies
every night under the glow of a tumescent
blue eye, over and over until, like falling,

she is caught in its cold soot-
stained gaze, is caught by its snare.

RAPTUS

What do I mean to say—
      Where I am is floating—
One foot tethered to Saturn's

      ring—the other chained
to the filth of the bedsheet's pull—
      Noosed by the fire of his skin—

I am an easy get—Hauled from
      my body—red-dark guilt
rises—poppies from loam—

      His naked incandescence—
my blue-black bruises—my force-
      flocked body—my dumb blue

tongue—I am lost in the unpeeling
      white crest of my skin—ash
stitched to my lashes—He looms—

      Swoops—a figure shrouded
in winter's wet kiss—He swells
      from the corners of this shrinking

room—The veins of his throat tighten—
      another seizure—The bed
is a swollen fist—is tooth and bone—

      I am thrown into the filth
kiln of his mouth—The girl with his soot-
      breath stench in her gut—

The girl cut open by his blood-licked
        tongue—What do I mean to say—
A gray fog is settled over my eyes—

    a clenched fist is bound
in my chest—These black moments—
        untrussed now—swim
in the pit of me—surface—wont drown.

A native of Chicagoland, **Elisa Karbin's** poems have appeared in such luminous venues as *Blackbird, Indiana Review, West Branch* and *Crab Orchard Review*. She has served as fiction editor for *cream city review* and contributing poetry editor for *New American Press* and *Great Lakes Review*. A passionate educator, she works as an academic consultant and has taught poetry enrichment courses for gifted teens and facilitated community poetry workshops. She currently teaches college composition and creative writing at the University of Wisconsin-Milwaukee, where she is finishing her PhD in poetry. She has two cats. Visit her online at www.elisakarbin.com.

www.ingramcontent.com/pod-product-compliance
Lightning Source LLC
LaVergne TN
LVHW041517070426
835507LV00012B/1632